Written by: LaShonda C. Henderson

ISBN-13: 978-0692706459
ISBN-10: 0692706453

Published by: Cshantay Publishing

Also by

LaShonda C. Henderson

Love and Other Thoughts

(A book of Poems and Love Quotes)

Love and Other Thoughts Journal

(A Journal to help Define individual Love)

Selah~ The Myth of Love Heart Changes

(A Novella)

Capturing Love's Light

(Poems and Prose)

LaShonda C. Henderson

Contents

The hardest part of Heartbreak was removing your clothes from my closet....

The roughest part of Heartbreak was putting your loving cards out of plain sight...

The cleansing part of heartbreak was replacing your memories with the truth...

The reality of heartbreak was loving my heart harder than any pain you caused me...

Welcome heartbreak old friend. When you come around, new love follows and takes me to heights unknown. So instead of heartbreak, we'll rename you "Heart Changes"

I thank you for the Lessons...

For my Community, may we heal.

Prologue

When I was a young girl, bath time was the only peaceful moment I would get. Growing up with two brothers and a sister, sharing one bathroom meant continuous chaos.

When everyone was distracted and the opportunity reared its head, I would fill the bathtub with water. Not just any water though; I always charged the water with energy; I used those rose scented, water softeners, the kind that fills the room and your soul with scent. But only when my Mom was not home, that way I had no tasks to interrupt the flow.

I would lavish in the silence and relax in the calm of the water, it was peace and I could be anything. The water brought me many imaginings.

I could be a mermaid or a deep-sea diver; whatever I could dream up in that quiet. My favorite thing involved pretending, that through my dainty petite legs, I was a Water Goddess. I could be in control; my motions could make me powerful, creating tidal waves at will. I would bend my knee to slide up and down the length of the tub, creating fragrant waves of water that moved hurriedly from one side to the next.

If I did it fast enough, spots in the tub, if only for a second, would reveal an empty, dry section where you could see the bottom. I would admire the movement, but mostly swell with pride at the strength of my legs. I thought how powerful my thighs must be to mimic a natural process that could knock out the strongest of men.

Yet my naivety did not prepare me for the real power these thighs could bring. Opening them to the wrong man can do just as much damage as any tidal wave approaching the shore, knocking many lives off their normal course. Yes, these thighs are powerful; they can destroy many lives if given at the wrong time to the wrong person. I Selah, stand as a witness to the pain thighs can cause in people's lives.

I have seen many thrown off course forever, due to the careless behavior of another person. I want you to understand, I had to become this observer. I am sharing so you gain some understanding, maybe you can even see another way. But I want to caution you, what I am telling you is not for you to judge the people. It is simply to help you understand that pain changes people. Sometimes forever.

Before I start, let me remind you that our people don't have a soft love. We never really have, as far as the generations I can remember or have heard about. We have a rough love, one just as passionate as we are. It looks different because it must be different. Slavery to freedom, Northerners to Southerners, Love Letters to Fist Fights, our love changed to meet our surroundings.

Oftentimes, it is for the better but most of the time, you'll see the product of the pain sauntering down the sidewalk, spewing its manifestations to every individual who crosses their path.

Yes, pain is an ingrained part of our society, yet, it does not have to end that way. We must discuss it, to address and change, so we can never thrive. I want to take you through a journey of

pain. However, do not dare say it was

not love; no matter how disruptive it

sounds.

Come with me………

FEAR

Keep walking, no looking back. I know you are tired but you must keep walking, don't give up babies.

I think to myself, "If I don't make it before this sun goes down, we may die." I must make it back to the city before nightfall. I cannot look back. These are the backwoods, we can't see the snakes if we cannot see the ground. However, I won't say it out loud, I can't tell my kids that, they have been through enough today.

He beat me in front of my kids. What type of man does that? He must be crazy. I must be crazy. My Daddy is going to kill this poor excuse for a man. Walking made my mind drift back to what just happened.

I scream as he hits me again. I do not know how many blows he has given me but I think I am going to pass out. The kids are screaming, their voices keep me conscious. I yell, I think I am yelling, be quiet I tell myself.

He is dragging me. The brush is ripping my skin the gravel is tearing my flesh. He's going to kill me; I know it, he's going to kill me.

"Baby you ok?" the older woman says with a voice of concern through a rolled down window. Her tone pulls me out of my thoughts. "Yes, I'm alive," why did I say that?

"Do you need a ride?" she urges with her voice.

I was so lost in my thought; I did not even notice her car. Much less, hear it slowing down on the roadway. We are walking on this soft shoulder and my mind is a million miles away.

"Yes, Ma'am" I say as I lower my head in shame, shrinking inside of myself at the sight she must see. A dirty woman; two small kids and no man walking hurriedly on this countryside; we must be a sight.

"Hop in" she says with a sign of relief in her voice.

I guide the children into the back seat and I sit in the front with her. I sit somberly, and glance back at my son and daughter. They are quiet, not quarreling as they usually do. They are still and quiet.

"Baby, you want to talk about it?" the woman says softly.

"No Ma'am" I utter, "thanks for the ride. You saved us a long walk."

"Where are, you headed?"

"Back to the city" I utter. Not ready to decide if I should go to my Father's house or my own.

Luckily, here, when we say "The City" all us country folks on this side of the county know what we mean. The city is where all the houses and commerce reside. I tell her, the city, so she understands that I just want to be where human life is after this day I have had.

She smiles and begins to drive her comfortable safe automobile.

The daylight is beginning to break the light from the sky; is acting like I feel right now inside, down. The sun is setting and my hopes of me and my man ever getting back together are going down too. He tried to kill me. Not just kill me; he tried to kill me in front of my kids in an isolated spot where no one would find me. How did we get to that place?

All I did was ask him, where he was. All I did was ask him, why Lucy felt like she could grin at me the way she did. I should be able to ask my husband that! I mean what is wrong with that? I am his wife; I am entitled to ask questions.

"Baby you sure you don't want to talk about it?" She breaks the conversation in my head.

I look at the backseat, and see my children sleeping. I burst into tears. I cannot help myself.

The woman pulls the car over to the side of the road. She reaches for me, and I shrink back.

"Aww Honey, I'm not here to harm you. I would never harm you." She coaxes.

Tears running down my face, dirt coating my hair, my skin bleeding from being drug along the coarse pavement, I melt into the seat a little.

"She reaches for my hand and strokes it softly. "Baby, I have seen many things in this life, but I haven't ever seen a man change unless he wanted to. A man did this to you didn't he."

I shook my head, still gasping for air while the tears fought for space on my cheeks.

"You ain't got to tell me, they think they own us." She sounded very haughty and angry.

"No, I made him do this." I stated firmly.

Looking at me all bewildered and confused. She took a deep breath. I could tell she was choosing her words carefully.

"You ain't did nothing." She said through clinched teeth, "that made you deserve THIS."

She points to me.

"Look at yourself", she reaches over, planting her hand on the roof of my side of the car, just above the windshield and thrust down. Still a little shaken from the events of the day, I bow my head.

"Look", she huffs.

Holding my head up, I notice a visor, the type with lights and a mirror, shining in front of me.

"You take a good look at your face." She says to me, sounding angry.

I hold my head up and see swollen eyes. The eyelids were not a normal pecan color of skin; instead, they displayed ones that were rapidly turning dark, like rotten meat. The complete left side of the face was large and protruding from its normal shape. Lips swollen, corners filled with dried blood, having burst open from the pressure of a fist.

My beautiful face lay open, broken pride scattered all over it like the remains of a battlefield. Like a war, I had lost terribly. No wonder my kids were crying so loudly. No wonder I felt so lost and outside of myself. He had beaten who I was away. My face was the proof of it. "That is not me", I thought.

Then suddenly, as I stared intently, those dark puffs began to ooze water, which turned into streaks of mud and blood. A mixture; of muck, that poured down that girl's face, the one in the mirror.

This cannot be real, that girl looks unloved and a horrid mess. That is not me. I reach up to my face, and that girl in the mirror echoes the same movement, I touched my eyes and winced from the pain, I stroked what could not be my cheek and felt tingles of pressure and pain.

My husband did this to that girl in the mirror. He did this to ME, his wife. All I did was ask a question.

Tears began rising from what felt like my stomach. I could feel; water, pain and energy coming up from the bottom of my body, out through these meat bags of eyes. He beat who I was away.

"You still ain't gone say nothing." She hissed.

"No Ma'am" I say. Still trying to process how that girl, that battered girl in THAT mirror in front of me could be the strong Woman that I am.

Ain't no way that's me.

Suddenly she slid over and hugged me. She grabbed me gently and hugged my doubt away.

That was I. That girl in the mirror is me. I am hurt. My face hurts and my pride is hurt. This stranger is holding me, hugging me as my husband's arms were supposed to do when I asked him those questions. This stranger is providing me comfort as I sit in her space broken physically and mentally. I am not a strong woman. I am that girl in the mirror. That poor broken girl. Poor me.

I pull back from her.

She looks at me knowingly and slides back to her side of the car back under the steering wheel. She hands me some tissue from a box on the floor and I mutter, "thank you" …between my gasps for air.

It hurts to breathe.

I glance in the mirror one more time. Looking closer at the damage, I could see my kids sound asleep in the back. I flip the mirror up and turn my head, to look at the setting sky, as she slowly pulls the car back on the road. Yes. He did this to me.

She breaks the monotony of the engine sound, bouncing through the car.

"Honey, I'm not going to tell you what to do with your life. But do you want to die?"

I swallow hard. I want to scream, I am already dead, look at me. My face, who I was, what I looked like is dead. My nose must be broken; my forehead filled with pain. The parts that make me, who I am, ARE already dead.

However, I mutter, "No, Ma'am".

Then, I am going to tell you some hard truth. Baby, I can see you have a ring on. I know that you are married and that you belong to him. Never the less, there ain't no shame in going back to your Daddy girl. You ain't got to lie and tell me that this is his first time, he's put his hands on you. Because baby where I just picked you up from, ain't nothing out here but crops and livestock.

"You all got farming plots out this way", she asked me; I could feel her looking over at me for an answer.

"No Ma'am," I said quietly.

I am going to tell you the truth, ask your Momma if you don't believe me.

"My Momma is dead," I interrupted.

"I'm sorry to hear that she said solemnly, changing her tone."

Baby, he did not bring you all the way out here with your kids to pick no crops.   You ain't out here to feed no

livestock.   Were   you   headed
somewhere?

"No Ma'am," I shook my head.

"He brought you out here to harm you. He wanted to hurt you, I cannot say what made him do it, now I don't know your situation, but I can say he has proven you are in danger."

I shifted in my seat and looked at her. She had to be at least 60, this woman is my elder and here she is telling me that MY husband wanted to harm ME.

"Are you saying that he?"

...I'm angry now...

"You do not know my husband, he chose me. He married ME, he loves ME."

The sound of movement in the back makes me stop speaking. I turn my head and see my son shifting in the seat, his eyes still closed.

Honey, ain't no love on your face. Did you see your face baby? That is all rage, and anger. I know it ain't my business. You are a woman, so your pain is MY pain. Baby, he hurt us.

I looked over, and noticed the tears streaming down her face.

What does she mean us? I'm the one sitting here with my face all distorted and body bruised, I'm the one whose husband just violated me because of stupid ass Lucy. There ain't no us. This woman is crazy.

I turn my head towards the window.

We make it towards the city and I decided. I was going home; back to my husband.

I break the silence by giving her the directions, telling her where to turn to get to my house.

She never said another word, after her tears started falling. She just drove.

We pull up to our house and my husband is standing outside smoking a cigarette. The woman stops the car. I get out and open the door; as I do, my husband walks towards the car.

"The kids are in the back," I say softly, but respectfully through my swollen lips.

He speaks to the woman. "Thank you for bringing them home Ma'am." Then he slides the kids out, one after the other, into his strong arms, the proof of their strength hidden all over my body, but displayed well on my face.

As I stand there, looking at his gentleness with the kids. He walks around to the driver's side of the car.

"Can I give you some gas money," he says to the woman.

Tears running down her face, she manages the words, "No that's ok" then easily, "I d-o n-o-t n-e-e-d a-n-y," oozes out of her mouth contempt vibrating into every syllable that she uttered.

He steps away from the car, looking defeated with the kids in his arms.

She pulls away.

He steps over to me, looking angry. "Did you tell her our business?" I walk slowly back into our house, holding the door open for him.

I will keep my mouth closed tonight.

Today taught me that I should keep it

closed tonight.

Reality

He tried to kill us.

Then I had to walk into school as if nothing happened. I do not even get to cry. I get to put on the brave face of, "At least I am here" and go on with life. That is what Momma said this morning. "At least we are alive."

I do not get to mourn for any part of me that dies every time the crazy begins to escalate. I do not get to cry and be comforted because the world definitely does not care. The world does not want to hear any sorrow from me. I am just a little girl. My wants fail to matter. If they did, that woman in that car would not have brought us back to that house; she would have taken us somewhere safe. Somewhere normal, where parents are not allowed to try and kill each other in front of their kids.

This world does NOT care.

Nobody cares about the wants of a child. Therefore, I sit here quietly in this classroom looking down at my class work. This world doesn't care. So, why should I?

When I grow up; ain't nobody ever going to be able to hurt me. I am going to marry the strongest man I can find. One who would beat Daddy up if he ever tried to hurt me like he does Momma. He is going to protect me. Unlike all these people in this, mean world.

"Come here," my teacher, yells out. Do you want me to call your Momma?

"No Ma'am," I utter.

Well stop staring into space and move your pencil. Do your work young lady.

"Yes Ma'am," I utter.

As I shuffle back to my desk, I hear giggles in the classroom.

Nope this world definitely doesn't care about a little girl like me. I begin to do my work silently.

The Truth

I lay still in my bed.

They are watching me; waiting for me to break down. I see it in their smirks when I cross over into their realm. That is why I hate to dream, I will not sleep willingly, I wait until my body forces it. I feel like the ancestors are waiting for me to crack.

They must whisper, "This is a strong one, we made her strong," as I rise to meet every challenge this life throws at me.

But, I am not.

I am a ticking time bomb waiting for the reason to act out on the pain that everyone heaped upon me. A childhood filled with violence; in my house, in my neighbor's houses, made me this way.

They say people like me turn to drugs and alcohol to release the pain, but not me. I want to face it head on. I want to see the result of the horror this community caused me. They broke me before any other race or societal group could. Do not talk to me about any oppressor outside of us.

No one could ever break me, because my family did that, they broke me before I could ever have a chance in the world...my family did that. They took away my ability to love and have a normal relationship. THEY DID THIS TO ME. Nope do not tell me about an oppressor other than the people who I watched, hold me down physically and mentally.

No child should ever have to sit and wonder is this the day we die? Is this the day that he decides to kill us?

The thoughts race in my mind as I lay in this bed. It always comes back to me during the darkness of the night. That day is stuck on repeat in my head. Who could ever forget the day the police came and took your Daddy? No one could forget about the day their Daddy went to jail.

She egged him on, I heard her shouting, "oh you're not a man you'll never do it. You're too weak to hurt anything."

I stood there, everything inside of me was screaming then; "he is already doing it Momma. He is hurting us every single day. Killing everything, I could ever want to be."

Maybe he heard it in my head shouting to his soul, I do not know. All I know is that right then, he did it. He killed her.

He killed my Momma.

All I could do was grab my brother's hand and sit there. Waiting for the only time when the world cared, when somebody died, to show up and act concerned.

He killed my Momma.

I sit here with my mind in the clouds reliving how this world doesn't care about me. How I watched, how no one saved my Momma. The community watched him kill her and the spirits of both her children.

I blame them for my brother being locked up now, he is an outcome, the residual pain. He is just like his Daddy, violent as hell.

My brother may have loved my Momma, but he never loved any women he lay with. He didn't love anybody. So, I can't say I was surprised when he went to jail like Daddy. What else was he supposed to do?

Violence in our house, and the community reinforced his behavior through every brawl. They chanted and high fived him for winning. He had to prove he was tough. He had to show them he wasn't no punk. Nobody respects a punk.

I sit here watching the stars, wondering. How do we get past this pain and heartbreak?

The ancestors must be watching and be very concerned, because no one in this world cares. They must be smirking, saying, "this one we made her strong."

But I am not.

I lay down to sleep and escape all chaos this world brings. The community killed me before I had a chance.

"This world doesn't care," I thought as I unwillingly closed my eyes from all this grief, this sorrow, this Pain.